FLAT STANLEY

Stanley in Space

Stanley in Space

Text copyright © 1990 by Jeff Brown
Illustrations by Macky Pamintuan, copyright © 2010 by HarperCollins Publishers
All rights reserved.

Published in agreement with the author, c/o BAROR INTERNATIONAL, INC., Armonk, New York, U.S.A. through
Danny Hong Agency, Seoul, Korea.

ISBN 979-11-93992-41-8 14740

Longtail Books

FLAT STANLEY

Stanley in Space

by Jeff Brown
Pictures by Macky Pamintuan

For Sidney Urquhart,
the godmother to whom Flat Stanley owes so much

CONTENTS

"Will you meet with us?

Does anyone hear?"

From the great **farness** of space,

from farther than any **planet** or

star that has ever been **mention**ed

in books, the questions came.

Again and again.

"Will you meet with us?

Does anyone hear?"

The Call

It was Saturday morning, and Mr. and Mrs. Lambchop were putting up **wallpaper** in the kitchen.

"Isn't this nice, George?" said Mrs. Lambchop, **stir**ring **paste**. "No excitement. A perfectly *usual* day."

Mr. Lambchop knew just what she meant. Excitement was often **troublesome**.

The flatness of their son Stanley, for example, after his big **bulletin board settle**d on him **overnight**. Exciting, but worrying too, till Stanley got round again. And that genie* visiting, **grant**ing wishes. Oh, very exciting! But all the wishes had to be *unwished* before the genie returned to the lamp from which he **sprung**.

"Yes, **dear**." Mr. Lambchop **smooth**ed down wallpaper. "**Ordinary**. The very best sort of day."

In the living room, Stanley Lambchop and his younger brother, Arthur, were watching a Tom Toad cartoon on TV. The **sporty** Toad was water-skiing* and fell off, making a great **splash**. Arthur laughed so hard he didn't hear the telephone, but

Stanley answered it.

"Lambchop **residence**?" said the caller. "The **President** of the United States speaking. Who's this?"

Stanley smiled. "The King of France."

"They don't have kings in France. Not anymore."

"Excuse me, but I'm too busy for **joke**s." Stanley **kept his eyes on** the TV. "My brother and I are watching the *Tom Toad Show*."

"Well, you *keep* watching, young

★ **genie** 지니. 아라비아 신화에 나오는 병이나 램프 속에 사는 요정.

✻ **water-ski** 수상 스키. 모터보트에 연결한 줄을 쥐고 보트에 이끌려 수면 을 활주하는 스포츠.

fellow!" The caller **hung up**, just as Mr. and Mrs. Lambchop came in to watch the **rest** of the show.

"Hey, guess what?" Stanley said.

"**Hay** is for horses," said Mrs. Lambchop, **mindful** always of careful speech. "Who called, dear?"

Stanley laughed. "The President of the United States!"

Arthur laughed too. "Stanley said *he* was the

King of France!"

Tom Toad **vanish**ed suddenly from the TV **screen**, and an American **flag** appeared. "We bring you a special message from the White House* in Washington, D.C.,*" said the deep voice of an **announcer**. "Ladies and gentlemen, the President of the United States!"

The screen showed the President,

★ **White House** 백악관. 미국의 대통령 관저.
✹ **Washington, D.C.** 워싱턴 D.C. 미국의 수도.

looking very serious, behind his desk.

"My fellow Americans," the President said. "I am sorry to **interrupt** this program, but someone out there doesn't **realize** that I am a very busy man who can't waste time joking on the telephone. I hope the **particular** person I am talking to—and I do *not* mean the King of France!—will remember that. Thank you. Now here's the Toad show again."

Tom Toad, still water-skiing, came back on the TV.

"Stanley!" **exclaim**ed Mrs. Lambchop. "The King of France indeed!"

"**Gosh**!" Arthur said. "Will Stanley get put in **jail**?"

"There is no law against being a

telephone **smarty**," Mr. Lambchop said. "Perhaps there should be."

The telephone rang, and he answered it. "George Lambchop here."

"Good!" It was the President. "I've been trying to **get hold of** you!"

"Oh, my!" Mr. Lambchop said. "Please excuse—"

"**Hold on**. You're the fellow has the boy was flat once, got his picture in the newspaper?"

"My son Stanley, Mr. President," Mr. Lambchop said, to let the others know who was calling.

"I had to be sure," said the President. "We have to get together, Lambchop! I'll send my **private** plane right now, **fetch** you all here to Washington, D.C."

Mr. Lambchop **gasp**ed. "Private plane? Washington? *All* of us?"

"The whole family." The President **chuckle**d. "**Including** the King of France."

Washington

At the White House, in his famous **Oval Office,*** the **President** shook hands with all the Lambchops.

"Thanks for coming." He **chuckle**d. "**Bet** you never thought when you woke up this morning that you'd get to meet me."

★**Oval Office** 백악관에 위치한 대통령 집무실. 방의 형태가 타원형(oval)이라 이렇게 부른다.

"Indeed not," Mr. Lambchop said. "This is quite a surprise."

"Well, here's another one," said the President. "The reason I asked you to come."

He sat down behind his desk, serious now. "Tyrra! Never heard of it, right?"

The Lambchops all shook their heads.

"*Nobody* ever heard of it. It's a **planet**, up there somewhere. They sent a message, the first ever from **outer space**!"

The Lambchops were greatly interested. "**Imagine**!" Mrs. Lambchop **exclaim**ed. "What did it say?"

"Very **friendly tone**," the President said. "**Peaceful**, just checking around. Asked us to visit. Now, my plan—"

A side door of the Oval Office had opened suddenly to **reveal** a nicely **dress**ed lady wearing a **crown**. Mrs. Lambchop **recognize**d her **at once** as the Queen of England.

"About the **banquet**, also the—" the Queen began, and saw that the President was busy. "Ooops! We **beg** your **pardon**." She closed the door.

"This place is a *madhouse*," the President said. "Visitors, **fancy** dinners, no end to it. Now, where—? Ah, yes! The *Star Scout!*"

He **lean**ed forward.

"That's our new top-secret **spaceship**, just ready now! Send somebody up in the *Star Scout*, I thought, to meet with these

Tyrrans. But who? Wouldn't look peaceful to send soldiers, or even scientists. Then I thought: What could be more peaceful than just an **ordinary** American boy?"

The President smiled. "Why not Stanley Lambchop?"

"Stanley?" Mrs. Lambchop **gasp**ed. "In a spaceship? To meet with an **alien race**?"

"Oh, boy!*" said Stanley. "I would love to go!"

"Me too," said Arthur. "It's not fair if—"

"Arthur!" Mr. Lambchop **drew in a** deep **breath**. "Mr. President, why *Stanley?*"

"It has to be someone who's already had **adventure** experience," the President

---

★ **boy** 여기에서는 '소년'이라는 뜻이 아니라, '맙소사!' 또는 '어머나!'라는 의미의 놀람·기쁨·아픔 등을 나타내는 표현으로 쓰였다.

said. "Well, my Secret Service* showed me a newspaper story about when Stanley was flat and caught two **rob**bers. Robbers! That's adventure!"

"I've had them too!" Arthur said. "A genie taught me to fly, and we had a Liophant, and—"

"A *what?*"

"A Liophant," Arthur said. "Half lion, half elephant. They're nice."

"Is that right? The Secret Service never—"

"Mr. President?" Mrs. Lambchop did not like to **interrupt**, but her **concern** was great.

---

*★ Secret Service 미국 대통령의 경호 기관.

"Mr. President?" she said. "This *mission*: Is it safe?"

"My **goodness**, of course it's safe!" the President said. "We have **take**n great **care**, Mrs. Lambchop. The *Star Scout* has all the **latest scientific equipment**. And it has been very carefully tested. First, we tried it on **automatic pilot**, with no **passenger**s. It worked perfectly! Even then, ma'am, we were not **satisfied**. We sent the *Star Scout* up again, this time with our **clever**est trained bird **aboard**. But hear for yourself." The President spoke into a little box on his desk. "Send in Dr. Schwartz, please."

A **beard**ed man entered, wearing a white coat and carrying a bird**cage** with a **cloth** over it. **Bow**ing, he removed the cloth to reveal a large, brightly colored **parrot**.

"Thank you, Herman," the President said. "Dr. Schwartz is our top space scientist," he told the Lambchops, "and this is Polly, the bird I spoke of. Polly, tell the **folk**s here about your adventure into space."

"**Piece of cake**," said the parrot. "**Terrific**! Loved every minute of it!"

"Thank you, Herman," the President said, and Dr. Schwartz carried Polly away.

"That was very **reassuring**, but it is **out of the question** for Stanley to go alone," Mrs. Lambchop said. "However, we were planning a family vacation. Would it be possible, Mr. President, for us all to go?"

"Well, if you don't mind the **crowd**ing,"

the President said. "And **skimp**ing on
baggage."

"Actually, we **had in mind** the **seaside**,"
Mr. Lambchop said. "Or a tennis camp.
But—"

The Queen of England looked in again.
"May we ask if—"

"Just a *minute*, for heaven's **sake**!" said the President.

"We shall return **anon**." Looking **peeved**, the Queen went away.

Mr. Lambchop had decided. "Mr. President, the seaside will keep. We will go to Tyrra, sir."

"Wonderful!" The President jumped up. "To the stars, Lambchops! Some training at the Space Center, and you're on your way!"

26

Taking Off

"Ten!" said the voice of **Mission** Control.

The **countdown** had begun. When it **reach**ed "zero," **Chief Pilot** Stanley Lambchop would **press** the "Start" button, and the *Star Scout* would **blast** off for Tyrra.

"Nine!"

Strapped into their seats, the

Lambchops **held their breath**s, each thinking very different thoughts.

Stanley was wondering if the Tyrrans would mind that Earth had sent just an ordinary family. Suppose they were big **stuck-up**s and **expect**ed a general* or a TV star, or even the President? Suppose—

"Eight!" said Control, and Stanley **fix**ed **his eyes on** the **panel** before him.

Mr. Lambchop was thinking that **serving** one's country was **noble**, but this was a bit much. How did these things happen? Off to an **unknown** planet, the **entire** family! Other families didn't have a

---

★ **general** 장군. 군대 계급 가운데 준장, 소장, 중장, 대장을 통틀어 이르는 말.

son become flat. Other families didn't find genies in the house. Other—Oh, well! Mr. Lambchop **sigh**ed.

"Seven!" said Control.

Mrs. Lambchop thought that Mr. Lambchop seemed **fretful**. But why, now that the *Star Scout* looked so *nice?* Thanks to her, in fact. "They may call it a **spaceship**," she had said when she first saw it, "but where's the *space?* Just one room! And all gray . . . ? **Drab**, I say!*" Much of the training at the Space Center, however, was **physical**, and Mrs. Lambchop, who **jog**ged and exercised

---

★**I say** 아이구! 어머나! 놀람이나 충격 등을 나타내는 표현.

regularly, quickly passed the tests **require**d. In the days that followed, while the others were being made **fit**, she used her free time to make the *Star Scout* more like home. Only so much **weight** was **permit**ted, but she managed a bathroom **scale** for the shower **alcove** and a plastic curtain, pretty **shade**s for the **porthole**s, a venetian **blind*** for the **Magnify**ing **Exploration** Window, and posters of Mexico and France.

"Six! . . . Five! . . . Four! . . . Three! . . ."

Mrs. Lambchop made sure her **purse** was **snug beneath** her seat.

---

* **venetian blind** 베니션 블라인드. 얇고 좁은 판을 일정한 간격으로 엮어 늘어뜨려 햇빛을 가리는 블라인드로, 통풍이 좋다.

Arthur, by **nature** lazy, was thinking that he was glad to be done with all the jogging, jumping, climbing **ladder**s, and scaling walls. When he was super-strong, thanks to the genie, it would have been easy. But for just **plain** Arthur Lambchop, he thought, it was **tiring**.

"Two!" said Control. "Good luck, everybody! One!"

"Pay **attention, dear**," Mrs. Lambchop told Stanley.

"Zero!" said Control, and Stanley pressed the "Start" button.

Whrooom! Rockets **roar**ing, the *Star Scout* rose from its **launch**ing **pad**.

Whroooooom! Whroooooom! **Gain**ing speed, it **soar**ed higher and higher,

32

carrying the Lambchops toward the
farness where Tyrra lay.

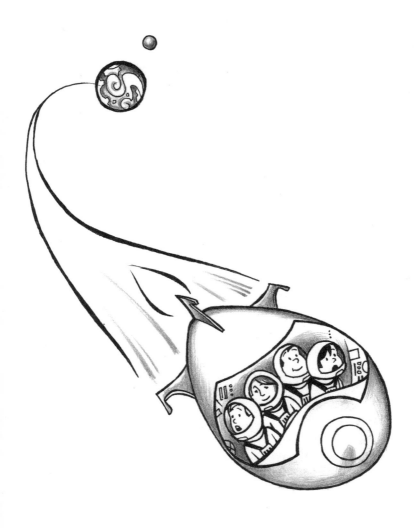

In Space

"I'll just **flip** this omelette," said Mrs. Lambchop, making breakfast in the *Star Scout*, "and then— Oh, dear!" The omelette **hover**ed like a Frisbee* in the air above her.

Mostly, however, after weeks in space, the Lambchops remembered that **gravity**,

---

★**Frisbee** 프리스비. 던지고 받는 놀이용 플라스틱 원반.

the **force** that held things down, did not exist beyond Earth's **atmosphere**. Mr. Lambchop often read now with his hands **clasp**ed behind his head, allowing his book to **float** before him, and Stanley and Arthur greatly enjoyed pushing from their chairs to **drift** like **feather**s across the room.

Raising her **pan**, Mrs. Lambchop brought down the omelette. "After breakfast, what?" she said. "A game of Monopoly?*"

"Please, not again." Arthur **sigh**ed. "If I'd known this **adventure** would be so **boring**, I'd never have come."

"The worst part," Stanley said, "is not

★**Monopoly** 모노폴리. 돈 모양의 종잇조각을 주고받으며 땅과 집을 사고 파는 놀이를 하는 보드 게임.

knowing how long it will **last**."

"The beginning wasn't boring," Arthur said as they began their breakfast. "The beginning was fun."

The first days had in fact been **tremendous**ly exciting. They had spent many hours at the *Star Scout*'s **Magnify**ing Window, watching the bright **globe** of Earth grow **steadily** smaller, until it seemed at last only a **pale marble** in the black of space. And there had been many special **sight**s to see: the **starry** beauty of the Milky Way,* the **planet**s—red Mars,*

★ **Milky Way** 은하. 천구(天球) 위에 구름 띠 모양으로 엷은 빛을 내며 길게 분포되어 있는 수많은 별들의 무리.

✳ **Mars** 화성. 태양계에서 4번째 궤도를 돌고 있으며 붉은 빛을 띠는 행성.

giant Jupiter,* cloudy Venus,* Saturn* with its shining rings.

The third evening they appeared on TV news **broadcast**s on Earth. Word of their **voyage** had been **release**d to the **press**, and all over the world people were eager to learn how this **extraordinary** adventure was **proceed**ing. Standing before the spaceship's camera, the Lambchops said they felt fine, looked forward to meeting the Tyrrans, and would **report** nightly while they remained in TV **range**.

The fourth evening they floated

★ **Jupiter** 목성. 태양계 내에 있는 행성 중에서 가장 큰 행성으로 행성의 순서 중 5번째에 위치하고 있다.

✳ **Venus** 금성. 태양계에 속하는 2번째 행성으로 지구에 가장 가까이 다가온다.

❋ **Saturn** 토성. 태양계의 6번째 행성으로 둘레에 아름다운 큰 고리 같은 테가 여러 개 있다.

before the camera, **demonstrating**
weightlessness. This was greatly
appreciated on Earth, and they floated
again the following day.

By the sixth evening, however,
they were **hard-pressed** to **liven** their
appearances. Mr. Lambchop **recite**d
a baseball **poem**, "Casey at the **Bat.***"

Stanley **juggle**d tennis balls, but the Earth audience, knowing now about weightlessness, saw the balls float when he **toss**ed them up. Arthur did **imitation**s of a **rooster**, a dog, and a man **stuck** in a phone **booth**. After this, while Mrs. Lambchop was singing her **college** song, he went behind the plastic curtain to un**dress** for a shower and **accidental**ly pulled the curtain down. He was **mortified**, and she tried later to **comfort** him.

"We will be remembered, Arthur, for our time in space," she said. "Nobody will care about a curtain."

"I will be remembered *forever*," Arthur

★**Casey at the Bat** Ernest L. Thayer가 쓴 '타석에 선 케이시'. 야구에서 영감을 받아서 쓴 시 가운데 가장 유명하다.

said. "A hundred million people saw me in my **underwear**."

The next day was Stanley's birthday, and just after dinner the **screen** lit up. There was the **President** in his **shirtsleeve**s, behind his desk in Washington, D.C.

"Well, here I am working late again," the President said. "It's a tough job, believe me. Happy birthday, Stanley Lambchop! I've **arrange**d a surprise. First, your friends from school."

There was silence for a moment, broken only by the **clear**ing of **throat**s, and then, from all the millions of miles* away, came the voices of Stanley's **classmate**s singing,

---

★**mile** 거리의 단위 마일. 1마일은 약 1.6킬로미터에 해당한다.

"Happy Birthday, dear Stanley! Happy Birthday to you!"

Stanley was tremendously **pleased**. "Thanks, everybody!" he said. "You too, Mr. President."

"That was just the U.S.A. part," said the President. "Ready over there in London, Queen?"

"We are indeed," the Queen's voice said **cheerful**ly. "And now, Master Lambchop, our famous Westminster Boys' **Choir**!"

From England, the beautiful voices of the famous choir sang "Happy Birthday, Stanley!" all over again, and then other children sang it from Germany, Spain, and France.

All this **attention** to Stanley made

Arthur **jealous**, and when the President
said, "By the way, Arthur, you **entertain**ed
us wonderfully the other night," he was
sure this was a **tease** about his appearance
in underwear. But he was wrong.

"Those imitations!" the President said.
"Especially the **fellow** in the phone booth.
Darn* good!"

"Indeed!" the Queen added from
England. "We were greatly **amuse**d."

"Oh, thank you!" said Arthur, **cheer**ed.
"I—"

The screen had gone **blank**.

They had traveled too far. There would
be no more voices from Earth, no voices

★ **darn** 말하는 내용을 강조하기 위해서 덧붙이는 'damn'을 순화한 단어로
'끝내주게'라는 뜻이다.

but their own until they heard what the Tyrrans had to say.

"Suppose the Tyrrans have forgotten we're coming?" Stanley said. "We might just **sail** around in space *forever.*"

They had finished the breakfast omelette, and were now setting out the Monopoly **board** because there was nothing more interesting to do.

"They don't even know our names," Arthur said. "What will they call us?"

"Earth people!" said a deep voice.

"Very probably," said Mr. Lambchop. "'Earth people' seems— Who said that?"

"Not me," said both Stanley and Arthur.

"Not *I*," said Mrs. Lambchop, correcting.

"But who—"

"Earth people!" The voice, louder now, came from the *Star Scout*'s radio. "**Greeting**s from the great planet Tyrra and its **mighty** people! Do you hear?"

"Oh, my!" Mr. Lambchop turned up the volume. "It's them!"

"*They*," said Mrs. Lambchop.

"For heaven's **sake**, Harriet!" Mr. Lambchop said, and spoke loudly into the microphone. "Hello, Tyrra. Earth people here. **Party** of four. Peace-loving family."

"Peace-loving?" said the voice. "Good! So is mighty Tyrra! Where are you, Earth people?"

Stanley checked his star maps. "We're just where the **tail** of Ralph's Comet* meets star number three million and forty-seven. Now what?"

"Right," said the Tyrran voice. "Keep going till you pass a star **formation** that looks like a foot. You can't miss it. Then, just past a **lopsided** little white moon, start down. You'll see a **pointy** mountain, then a big **field**. **Land** there. See you soon, Earth people!"

"You **bet**!" Mr. Lambchop said, and turned to his family. "The first **contact** with another planet! We are making history!"

They passed the foot-shaped star formation, then the lopsided moon, and

★ comet 혜성. 가스 상태의 빛나는 긴 꼬리를 끌고 태양을 초점으로 긴 타원이나 포물선에 가까운 궤도를 그리며 운행하는 천체.

Stanley piloted the *Star Scout* down.
The darkness of space **vanish**ed as it
descended, and at last the Lambchops saw
clearly the planet it had taken so long to
reach.

Tyrra was smallish as planets
go, but nicely round and
quite pretty, all in **shade**s of
brown with **marking**s not
unlike the oceans and

continents of Earth. A pointy mountain came into sight, and beyond it a big field.

"There!" Stanley pressed the button, "Landing."

Whrooom! went the *Star Scout*'s rockets. The spaceship hovered, then touched down.

Peering out, the Lambchops saw only a brown field, with tan★ trees at the far side

---

★tan 황갈색. 검은 빛을 띤 누른 빛을 말한다.

and **brownish** hills beyond.

"**Curious**," said Mr. Lambchop. "Where are—"

Suddenly a message came, but not the sort they **expect**ed.

"**Surrender**, Earth people!" said the radio. "Your spaceship is **trap**ped by our un**breakable** trapping **cable**! You are **prisoner**s of Tyrra! Surrender!"

The Tyrrans

Unbreakable trapping cable? Prisoners? Surrender? The Lambchops could **scarcely** believe their ears.

"I don't call *that* **peaceful**," said Mrs. Lambchop. "Our President has been **misled**."

"I wish we had gone to the **seaside**." Mr. Lambchop shook his head. "But *how* are we trapped? I don't—" He pointed to the

Magnifying Window. "What's that?"

A **thin** blue line, like a **thread**, had been passed over the *Star Scout*. Stanley **switch**ed **on** the **wiper** above the big window and the first **flick** of its **blade** **part**ed the blue line.

"Drat!*" said the radio.

Other voices rose, **startled**, and then the deep voice spoke again. "Earth people! We're sending a **messenger**! A regular, **ordinary** Tyrran, just to show what we're like."

For long moments, the Lambchops **kept their eyes on** the tan trees across the **field**.

"There!" Arthur said suddenly. "Coming

★ drat 제기랄! 젠장!

toward— Oh! Oh, my . . ." His voice **trail**ed **away**.

The Tyrran messenger came slowly forward to stand before the big window, a **muscular**, **scowl**ing young man with a **curl**ing **mustache**, wearing shorts and carrying a **club**.

The mustache was very large. The messenger was not.

"That man," Mrs. Lambchop said slowly, "is only three inches* tall."

"At most," Mr. Lambchop said. "It is a magnifying window."

The Tyrran seemed to be calling something. Arthur opened the door a

---

★ inch 길이의 단위 인치. 1인치는 2.54센티미터이다.

crack, and the words came clearly now. ". . . afraid to let us see you, Earth people? Because I'm so **enormous**? Hah! *All* Tyrrans are this big!"

Flinging the door wide, Arthur showed himself. "Well, I'm a *small* Earth person!" he shouted. "The **rest** are even bigger than me!"

"*I*, not me," Mrs. Lambchop said. "And don't **tease**, Arth— Oh! He's **faint**ed!"

Wetting her **handkerchief** with cold water, she jumped down from the *Star Scout* and ran to **dab** the Tyrran's **tiny brow**.

Cries rose again from the **spaceship**'s radio. "A giant killed Ik! . . . There's another, even bigger! . . . Oh, **gross**! . . . Look! Ik's all right!"

The Tyrran, by **grasp**ing Mrs. Lambchop's handkerchief, had indeed pulled himself up. **Furious**, he **swung** his club, but managed only to **tap** the top of her shoe. "**Ouch! Scat!**" she said, and he **dart**ed back across the field.

"Oh, my!" said the radio. "**Never mind** about surrendering, Earth people! A **truce committee** is on the way!"

At first they saw only a tiny **flag**, **flutter**ing like a white butterfly far across the brown field, but at last the Tyrran committee drew close, and the Lambchops, waiting now outside the *Star Scout*, could **make** each little person **out**.

The flag was carried by the scowling

young man with the mustache and the club. The other members of the committee, a bit smaller even than he, were a red-faced man wearing a **uniform** with medals across the chest, a **stout** lady in a yellow dress and a hat with flowers on it, and two older men in blue **suit**s, one with **wavy**

white hair, the other thin and **bald**.

The committee **halt**ed, **staring** bravely up.

"I am General Ap!" shouted the uniformed man. "**Commander** of all Tyrran **force**s!"

Stanley stepped forward. "**Chief Pilot** Stanley Lambchop," he said. "From Earth. These are my parents, Mr. and Mrs. George Lambchop. And my brother, Arthur."

"President Ot of Tyrra, and Mrs. Ot," said General Ap, **indicating** the wavy-haired man and the lady. "The bald **chap** is Dr. Ep, our scientist. The **grouchy** one with the flag is my **aide**, Captain* Ik."

★ **captain** 대위. 군대 계급 가운데 하나로 초급 장교 중 가장 높다.

No one seemed sure what to say next. A few **polite remark**s were exchanged— "Nice meeting you, Earth people!" . . . "Such a pretty planet, Tyrra!" . . . "Thank you. Were you very long in space?"—and Mr. Lambchop **realize**d suddenly that the Tyrrans were uncomfortable talking almost straight up. He got down on his **knee**s, the other Lambchops **followed his example**, and the Tyrrans **at once lower**ed their heads in **relief**.

"Right!" said General Ap. "All **reasonable** people here! A truce, eh?"

"I'm for war, **frankly**," **growl**ed Captain Ik, but Stanley pretended not to hear. "A truce? Good idea," he said. "We come in peace."

Mrs. Ot **sniff**ed. "Not very peaceful, **frighten**ing poor Captain Ik." She pointed at Arthur. "That giant shouted at him!"

"My son is not a giant," Mrs. Lambchop said. "It's just that you Tyrrans are—how to put it?—unusually *petite*."

"Ik's the biggest we've got, actually," said General Ap. "We hoped he'd **scare** you."

President Ot raised his hand. "No **harm** done! Come! TyrraVille, our **capital**, is but a **stroll** away."

The Lambchops, **equip**ped now with **handy** magnifying lenses from the *Star Scout*'s science **kit**, followed the committee.

TyrraVille lay just across the brown field, behind the tan trees, no larger than an Earth-size tennis **court**.

TyrraVille

"**Gosh!**" Stanley said. "It makes me **homesick**, in a way."

Except for its size, and the **lack** of greenness, the Tyrran **capital** was indeed much like a small village on Earth. A Main Street **bustle**d with Tyrrans shopping and running **errand**s; there were handsome school and public buildings, two churches with **spire**s as high as Mr. Lambchop's **waist**, and **side street**s of pretty houses with **lawn**s like **neat** brown **postage stamp**s.

Captain Ik, still angry, **march**ed on ahead, but the **rest** of the **committee halt**ed at the head of Main Street.

"We'll just show you *around*, eh?" said **President** Ot. "Safer, I think."

The Lambchops saw at once the **risk** of walking streets **scarcely** wider than their feet. **Escort**ed by the committee, they **circle**d the little capital, **bend**ing often to make use of their **magnify**ing lenses. Mrs. Ot **took care** to **indicate** points of **particular** interest, among them Ux Field, a sports center, Admiral* Ux **Square**, Ux

Park, and the Ux Science Center Building.
("Mrs. Ot's grandfather," **whisper**ed
General Ap. "Very rich!")

The tour caused a great **stir**. Everywhere
the **tiny citizen**s of TyrraVille **wave**d from
windows and **roof**tops. At the Science
Center, the last stop, **journalist**s took
photographs, and the
Lambchops were **treat**ed
to Grape Fizzola, the
Tyrran national
drink, hundreds of
bottles of which were
emptied into four **tub**s to
make Earth-size **portion**s.

★ **Admiral** 제독. 해군의 함대사령관 또는 해군장성에 대한 통칭.

Refreshed by his Fizzola, Arthur took a little run and **hurdle**d a large part of TyrraVille, **land**ing in Ux Square. "Arthur!" Mrs. Lambchop **scold**ed, and he hurdled back.

"Aren't kids the dickens?*" said a Tyrran mother, **look**ing **on**. "Mine—Stop *tugging*, Herbert!" These last words seemed **address**ed to the ground beside her. "My youngest," she explained.

Stanley **squint**ed. "I can **hardly**—He's just a *dot*."

"Dot yourself!" said an angry voice. "Big-a-rooney! *You're* the funny-looking one!"

★ dickens 개구쟁이.

65

"Herbert!" his mother said. "It is rude to **make fun of** people for their shape or size!"

"As I said myself, often, when Stanley was flat!" Mrs. Lambchop **exclaim**ed. "If only—"

"**Surrender**, Earth people!"

The cry had come from Captain Ik, who appeared now from behind the Science Center, **stagger**ing **beneath** the **weight** of a boxlike machine almost as big as he was, with a **tube stick**ing **out** of it.

"Surrender!" he shouted. "You cannot **resist** our Magno-Titanic **Paralyze**r **Ray**! Tyrra will yet be saved!"

"There's a **truce**, Ik!" **bark**ed General Ap.
"You can't—"

"Yes, I can! First— Ooops!" Captain
Ik's **knee**s had **buckle**d, but he **recover**ed
himself. "First I'll paralyze the one who
scared me back there in the field!"

Yellow light **flicker**ed up at Arthur from
the Magno-Titanic Paralyzer.

"**Yikes!**" said Arthur, as **shriek**s rose
from the **crowd**.

But it was not on Arthur that the
Magno-Titanic **beam** landed. Stanley had
sprung forward to **protect** his brother,
and the light shone now on his chest and
shoulders. Mrs. Lambchop almost **faint**ed.

Suddenly her **fright** was gone.

Stanley was smiling. The yellow rays

still flickering upon him, he **roll**ed his head and **wiggle**d his hands to show that he was fine. "It's nice, actually," he said. "Like a massage."

The crowd **hoot**ed. "It only works on people Tyrran-size!" someone called. "You're a **ninny**, Ik!" Then Captain Ik was marched off by a Tyrran policeman, and the crowd, still laughing, **drift**ed away.

Mrs. Lambchop spoke **stern**ly to the committee. "'Tyrra will yet be saved'? What did Captain Ik mean? And why, **pray** tell, did he **attempt** to paralyze my son?"

The Ots and General Ap exchanged **glance**s. Dr. Ep **stare**d at the ground.

"Ah!" said President Ot. "Well . . . The fact is, we're having a . . . A **crisis**, actually. Yes. And Ik, well, he, ah—"

"Oh, tell them!" Mrs. Ot **burst** suddenly into tears. "About the Super-Gro! Tell, for heaven's **sake**!"

Puzzled, the Lambchops stared at her. The sky had **darken**ed, and now a light rain began to fall.

"Wettish, eh?" said General Ap. "Can't offer **shelter**, I'm afraid. No place large enough."

"The *Star Scout* will do nicely," said Mrs. Lambchop. "Let us return to it for tea."

President Ot's Story

"Tea *does* help. I am quite myself again."
Mrs. Ot **nod**ded to her husband. "**Go on, dear**. Tell."

Rain **drum**med **faint**ly on the *Star Scout*, making even **cozier** the **scene** within. About the dining table, the Lambchops **occupied** their usual places. The Tyrrans sat **atop** the table

on **thumbtack**s pushed down to **serve** as **stool**s, **sip**ping from tiny cups Mrs. Lambchop had **fashion**ed from aluminum foil,* and **nibbling crumb**s of her homemade ginger snaps.*

Now, **sigh**ing, President Ot set down his cup.

"You will have **observe**d, Lambchops," he said, "how greatly we have enjoyed these tasty **refresh**ments. The fact is, Tyrra has for some time been totally without fresh food or water **fit** to drink. We live now only by what **tin**s and bottles we **had in store**."

★ **aluminum foil** 은박지. 포장 재료, 단열재 그리고 전선, 전기부품 등에 쓰인다.

✳ **ginger snap** 생강 쿠키. 생강과 당밀로 맛을 낸 작고 얇은 쿠키.

Mrs. Ot **made a face**. "Pink meat **spread**s, and **spinach**. And that *dreadful* Fizzola."

"A bit sweet, yes," said General Ap. "Gives one gas, too. But—"

"**Never mind!**" cried Mrs. Ot.

President Ot continued. "The cause of our **tragedy**, Lambchops, was Super-Gro. An **invent**ion of Dr. Ep's. Super-Gro, Ep promised, would **double** our **crop**s, make them double size, double delicious as well. A great concept, he said."

"We scientists," said Dr. Ep, "dream larger than other men."

"For three days, at the Science Center," President Ot went on, "Ep **brew**ed his Super-Gro. Great **smelly vat**s of it, enough

74

for the whole **planet**. But then . . . Oh, no

Tyrran will ever forget that fourth day!

I myself was **stroll**ing through Ux Park.

How beautiful it was! The trees and grass

so green, the sky—"

"Green?" said Arthur. "But everything's

brown here, not green!"

"A **mishap**," **murmur**ed Dr. Ep. "With

the Super-Gro."

"Mishap?" **bark**ed General Ap. "The

stuff *exploded*, Ep! All over the place!"

"Well, nobody's perfect." Dr. Ep **hung**

his head.

"All those huge vats, Lambchops!"

President Ot continued. "**Boom**! One

after another! **Shatter**ed windows, blew

the **roof** off the Science Center! No one

hurt, **thank goodness**, but great clouds of smoke, **darken**ing the sky! And then—such dreadful luck!—it began to rain. A *tremendous* rain, mixing with the smoke, falling all over Tyrra, into the rivers, on to every **field** and garden, every bit of **greenery**."

Rising from his thumbtack, he **pace**d **back and forth** across the table.

"When the rain stopped, there was no green. None. Just brown. Worse, Ep's tests **prove**d that our water was undrinkable, and that nowhere on Tyrra would anything grow. I **broadcast at once** to the nation. 'Do not **despair**,' I said, 'Tyrra will soon **recover**.'"

"Oh, good!" Mr. Lambchop said.

President Ot shook his head. "I lied. I couldn't tell the truth, for fear of causing **panic**, you see. The tests showed that it would be a year at least before Tyrra was green again. And long before that we will

have emptied our last tin, our last bottle of Fizzola."

He sat down again, covering his face with his hands.

"So then we . . . We sent a message, into space. **Lure** some other planet's **spaceship**, we thought. Hold it for **ransom**, you see, make them send food and water. Oh, **shameful**! **Underhand**ed. You will never forgive us, I know . . ."

His voice **trail**ed **away**, and there was only the **patter** of the rain.

Close to tears, the Lambchops looked at each other, then at the little people on the tabletop. The Tyrrans seemed **particular**ly tiny now, and brave, and nice.

"You poor dears!" Mrs. Lambchop said.

"There was no need to *conquer* us. We would help you **willing**ly, if we could."

The Tyrrans seemed at first unable to believe their ears. Then, suddenly, their faces shone with joy.

"**Bless** you!" cried General Ap.

"Saved!" Mrs. Ot **clap**ped her hands. "We are saved!"

"Saved . . . ?" said Mrs. Lambchop.

"Of course!" said President Ot. "Don't you see? Earth's spaceships can bring food and water till— Oh! What's wrong?"

It was Arthur who explained.

"I'm very sorry," he said. "But there's just the *Star Scout*. Earth hasn't got any other spaceships. And it would take years to build them."

The Tyrrans **gasp**ed. "Years . . . ?" said Dr. Ep.

Stanley felt so sad he could **hardly** speak. "And it's no use going for food in the *Star Scout*," he said. "By the time we returned from Earth, you'd all be— Well, you know."

"Dead," said Mrs. Ot.

In the *Star Scout*, a **terrible** silence fell. The facts were clear. The **cupboard**s of Tyrra would soon be empty. And then all its tiny people would **starve** to death.

Stanley's Good Idea

The tea**pot** was cold now, and a last cookie **crumb** lay unwanted on a **plate**. **Gloom** hung like a dark cloud within the *Star Scout*.

"It's not fair," Arthur said for the third time. "It's just not."

"Stop saying that," Stanley told him. "That's four times now."

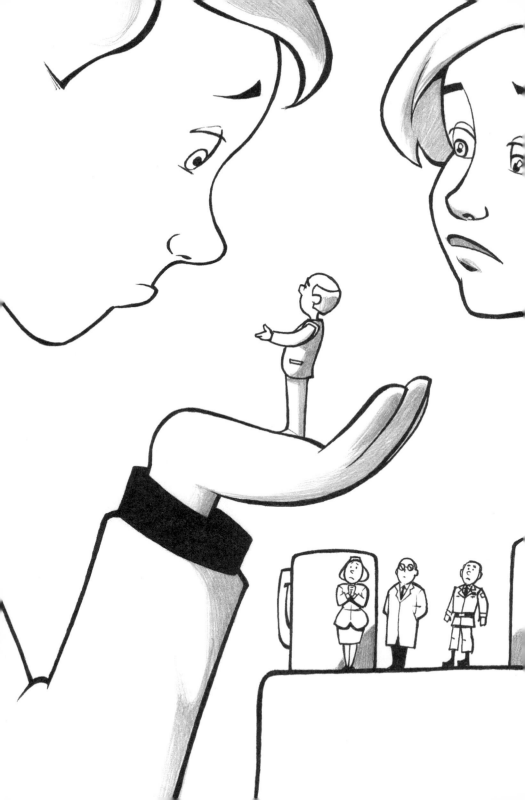

"Five," said Dr. Ep.

General Ap tried to be **cheerful**. "Ah, well . . . Still some **tin**ned meat, eh? And **plenty** of Grape Fizzola. Much to be **thankful** for."

"I will *never* be thankful for Grape Fizzola," said Mrs. Ot.

"It's just that . . ." Arthur sighed. "I mean, Earth has so *much* food. Millions of people, and there's mostly still enough."

The Tyrrans seemed **amaze**d. "Millions? You're **joking**?" said **President** Ot.

"Hah!" said General Ap. "**Dreadful crush**, I should think. Millions?"

Mrs. Lambchop smiled. "With all our great nations, many millions. And still the numbers grow."

"Well, here too." President Ot shook his head. "**Youthful marriage**s, babies one after another. But *millions?* Our **population**—there's just TyrraVille, of course—is six hundred and eighty-three."

"Eighty-four," said Mrs. Ot. "Mrs. Ix had a baby last night."

Now it was the Lambchops who were amazed.

"Just TyrraVille?" Arthur cried. "But TyrraVille's your *capital*, you said!"

"Well, it would have to be, wouldn't it, dear?" said Mrs. Ot.

Stanley shook his head. "On the whole planet, only six hundred and eighty-four Tyrrans! **Gosh**, I'll **bet**—Wait!"

An idea had come to him. Stanley had

had exciting ideas before, but none that excited him as much as this one did.

"Mrs. Ot!" he shouted. "How much do you **weigh**?"

"Stanley!" said Mrs. Lambchop.

Mrs. Ot was not **offend**ed. "Actually,

I've **slim**med a bit. Though not, sadly, in the **hip**s. I'm six ounces,* young man. Why do you ask?"

The words **rush**ed out of Stanley. "Because if you're **average**, only children would be even lighter, then all the Tyrrans **put together** would weigh—Let me **figure** this **out**!"

"Less than three hundred pounds,*" said Mr. Lambchop, who was good at math. "Though I don't see—" Then he did see. "Oh! Good for you, Stanley!"

"The **lad**'s bright, we know," said General Ap. "But what—"

★ **ounce** 무게의 단위 온스. 1온스는 약 28.35그램이다.
✳ **pound** 무게의 단위 파운드. 1파운드는 약 0.45킬로그램이다.

"General!" said Mr. Lambchop.
"**Summon** all Tyrrans here to the *Star Scout!* **Fetch** what **remain**s of your tinned food and Grape Fizzola! Perhaps Earth can be your home till Tyrra is green again!"

The Weighing

From each little house on each little street, the Tyrrans came, every man, woman, and child, even Captain Ik with a **guard** from the **jail**. The rain had stopped, and the evening light shone gold on the brown **field** in which the **tiny** people stood **assemble**d.

President Ot **address**ed them. "**Fellow**

Tyrrans! I must **confess** that your government has **deceive**d you! The truth is: It will be at least a year before our fields and **stream**s are **fit** again."

Cries rose from the **crowd**. "We were lied to!" . . . "**Lordy, talk about** bad news!" . . . "We'll **starve!**" . . . "Shoot the scientists!"

"Wait!" shouted President Ot. "We are offered **refuge** on Earth, if the **voyage** is possible! Pay **attention**, please!"

Stepping forward, Mr. Lambchop read aloud from the **booklet** that had come with the *Star Scout*.

"'Your spacecraft has been **design**ed for safety as well as **comfort**. Use only as directed.'" He raised his voice. "'Do not add **weight** by bringing **souvenirs aboard** *or by inviting friends to ride with you.'*"

Cries rose again. "That did it!" . . . "We're not *souvenirs!*" . . . "He said no friends either, stupid!" . . . "We**'ve had it**, looks like!"

Mr. Lambchop raised his hand. "There is still hope! But you must all be weighed! Also the **supplies** you would **require** for the trip!"

The *Star Scout*'s bathroom **scale**, set down in the field, **prove**d too high for the Tyrrans, and the weighing was **brief**ly **delay**ed until Arthur, using the Monopoly **board**, made a **ramp** by which they could easily **mount**.

General Ap **bark**ed orders. "Right, then!

Groups of twenty to twenty-five, families together! And don't **jiggle**!"

The Ots and six other families **march**ed up onto the scale, beside which Mrs. Lambchop stood with **pad** and pencil. "Seven and one-quarter pounds!" she said, writing it down.

"Next!" shouted General Ap, but the Ot group was already starting down, and another marching up.

Group after group mounted the scale. There *was* jiggling, due to excited children, but Mrs. Lambchop **took care** to wait until the **needle** was **still**. Within an hour the **entire population** of Tyrra had been weighed, along with its supplies of **tin**ned food and Fizzola, and she added up.

"Tyrrans, two hundred and thirty-nine," she **announce**d. "Food and Fizzola, one hundred and forty. Total: Three hundred and seventy-nine pounds!"

"Are we saved? Or are we too fat?" came a cry.

"Too soon to tell!" Mr. Lambchop called back. "We must see how we can **lighten** our ship!"

A good start was made by **discard**ing the *Star Scout*'s dining table and one steel **bunk**, since Stanley and Arthur could easily share. Then out went Stanley's tennis balls, extra sweater, and his **Chief Pilot zip** jacket with the American **flag**; out went Arthur's **knee** socks,* raincoat,* and a plastic **gorilla** he had **smuggle**d aboard. Mr. and Mrs. Lambchop added their extra clothing, lamps, **kitchenware**, the Monopoly game, and at last, the posters of Mexico and France.

The crowd stood **hush**ed as the **pile** was weighed. Somewhere a baby cried, and its parents **scold**ed it.

"Three hundred and seventy-seven pounds!" Mrs. Lambchop announced. "Oh, **dear**!" she **whisper**ed to President Ot. "Two less than we need."

"I see." President Ot, after a moment's thought, climbed up onto the scale. "Good

---

★ **knee socks** 무릎까지 오는 양말.
✳ **raincoat** 비나 눈이 내릴 때 의복을 보호하기 위하여 착용하는 방수용 코트.

95

news, Tyrrans!" he called. "Almost all of us are saved!"

Cheers went up, and then someone shouted, "What do you mean, *almost* all?"

"We weigh, as a nation, a bit too much," President Ot explained. "But only four, if largish, need stay behind. I shall be one. Will three more **volunteer**?"

Murmurs rose from the crowd. "That's *my* kind of President!" . . . "Leave Ik behind!" . . . "How about you, Ralph?" . . . "Ask somebody else, darn you!"

The matter was quickly **resolve**d. "I won't go without you, dear," Mrs. Ot told her husband, and Captain Ik, hoping to **regain popularity**, announced that he too would remain.

General Ap was the fourth volunteer. "Just an old soldier, ma'am," he told Mrs. Lambchop. "Lived a full life, time now to just **fade** away, to—"

"Hey! Wait!"

Arthur was pointing to the scale.

"We forgot *that*," he said. "We can leave the scale behind. Now nobody has to stay!"

Heading Home

"Mr. and Mrs. Ix, and the new baby?" said **President** Ot, beside his wife on a **ledge** above the **Magnify**ing Window. "Ah, yes, on the **fridge**!"

The people of Tyrra were being made as comfortable as possible in the various **nook**s and **crannies** of the *Star Scout*. Stanley and Arthur had cleared

a **cupboard** where Tyrra High School students could study during the trip, and Mrs. Lambchop had cut up **sheet**s to make hundreds of little **blanket**s, and put out bits of cotton* for **pillow**s. "**Makeshift**, Mrs. Ix," she said now, **settling** the Ixes on the fridge. "But *such* short **notice**. Back a bit from the **edge**, yes?"

"Short notice indeed," said Mrs. Ix. "So many—"

"Not to worry." Mrs. Lambchop smiled proudly. "My son, the **Chief Pilot**, will call ahead."

From a nearby **shelf**, Captain Ik

★ cotton 솜. 목화씨에 달라붙은 털 모양의 흰 섬유질. 부드럽고 가벼우며 흡습성, 보온성이 있다.

✳ thee 목적격 대명사 'you(너를)'의 고어.

whispered an **apology** for **attempt**ing to **paralyze** Arthur. "Between you and I, I didn't really think it would work," he said.

"Between you and *me*," said Mrs. Lambchop. "But thank you, Captain Ik." She turned to Stanley. "We're all ready, **dear**!"

Stanley checked his controls. "Let's go!"

"Tyrrans!" President Ot called for **attention**. "Our national **anthem**!"

Everywhere in the *Star Scout*, Tyrrans rose, their right hands over their hearts. "*Hmmmm . . .*" **hum**med Mrs. Ot, setting a **key**, and they began to sing.

"Tyrra, the lovely! Tyrra, the free!
*Hear, dear **planet**, our promise to thee!***

Where e'er we may go, where e'er we may
roam,
We'll come back to Tyrra, Tyrra our home!"

The words **echo**ed in the softly lit
cabin. Many Tyrrans were **weep**ing, and
the eyes of the Lambchops, as they took
their seats, **glisten**ed too.

*"Be it ever so **humble**, there's no planet so
dear,*
We'll always love Tyrra, from far or from—"

Stanley **press**ed the "Start" button,
and—*Whroooom!*—the *Star Scout*'s rockets
roared to life.
The singing stopped suddenly, and Mrs.

Ix cried out from the fridge. "Oh, my! Is this thing safe?"

"Yes indeed," Mrs. Lambchop called back.

"Perhaps," said Mrs. Ix. "But it is my belief that if Tyrrans were meant to fly, we'd have wings."

Whroooom! Whroooom!

The *Star Scout* lifted now, **gain**ing speed as it rose. Its **mission** was done. The strangers who had called from a **distant** planet were no longer strangers, but friends.

It was all very **satisfactory**, Stanley thought. The other Lambchops thought so too.

Earth Again

". . . real **pleasure** to welcome you, Tyrrans," said the **President**, almost done with his speech. "I wish you a fine year on Earth!"

Before him on the White House **lawn**, with newspaper and TV **reporter**s all about, sat the Lambchops and, in a **tiny grandstand** built especially for the

occasion, the people of Tyrra.

The Tyrrans were now **applaud**ing **polite**ly, but they looked nervous, and Mrs. Lambchop guessed why. That **crowd** at the Space Center for the *Star Scout's* **land**ing, that drive through crowded streets into Washington, D.C.! Poor Tyrrans! Everywhere they looked, giant buildings, giant people. How could they feel comfortable here?

But a surprise **was in store**. Across the lawn, a great white **sheet** had been **spread**. Now, at the President's **signal**, workmen pulled the sheet away.

"Welcome," said the President, "to TyrraVille Two!"

Gasps rose from the Tyrrans, then

shouts of joy.

Before them, on what had been the White House tennis **court**, lay an **entire** village of tiny houses, one for each Tyrran family, with shops and schools and churches, and a **miniature railway serving** all **principal** streets. Begun when Stanley called ahead from space, TyrraVille Two had been completed well before the *Star Scout*'s arrival, thanks to **rush deliver**ies from **leading** toy stores in Washington and New York.

The excited Tyrrans ran from the grandstand to **explore** their new homes, and soon happy voices rose from every window and **doorway** of TyrraVille Two. "Nice **furniture!**" . . . "**Hooray**! Fresh lemonade! No more Fizzola!" . . . "In the **cupboard**s, see? Shirts, dresses, **suit**s, shoes!" . . . "**Underwear**, even!"

The Ots, General Ap, Dr. Ep, and Captain Ik came back to say good-bye, and the Lambchops **knelt** to touch **fingertip**s in **farewell**. The TV men filmed this, and Arthur made everyone laugh, pretending to be **paralyze**d by the touch of Captain Ik. Then the newsmen left, the Tyrrans returned to TyrraVille Two, and only the President remained with the Lambchops on the White House lawn.

"Well, back to work." The President **sigh**ed. "Good-bye, Lambchops. You're all heroes, you know. Saved the nation."

"Not really," Stanley said. "They

couldn't have **conquer**ed us."

"Well, you know what I mean," the President said. "You **folk**s care to stay for **supper**?"

"Thank you, no," Mrs. Lambchop said. "It is quite late, and this has been an exciting but very **tiring** day."

It was **bedtime** when they got home. Stanley and Arthur had a light supper, with hot chocolate to help them sleep, after which Mr. and Mrs. Lambchop **tuck**ed them in and said good night.

The brothers lay quietly in the darkness for a moment. Then Arthur **chuckle**d.

"The Magno-Titanic Paralyzer *was* sort of **scary**," he said. "You were brave,

Stanley, **protect**ing me."

"That's okay," Stanley said. "You're my brother, right?"

"I know . . ." Arthur was sleepy now. "Stanley? When the Tyrrans go back, will their land and water be okay? Will they let us know?"

"I guess so." Stanley was **drowsy** too. "Good night, Arthur."

"Good night," said Arthur, and soon they were both asleep.

And **in time**, from the great **farness** of space, but a farness no longer strange or **unknown**, another message came.

"We are home. All is well."

And again.

"We are home! Thank you, Earth!

All is well!"

The End